Among Ruins

CHRISTOPHER DODA

Among Ruins

The **Mansfield** Press

Canadian Cataloguing in Publication Data

Doda, Christopher, 1971-
      Among Ruins

Poems

ISBN 1-894469-04-6

1. Title
PS8557.O2245A8 2001   C811'.6   C2001-901884-3
PR9199.4.D63A8 2001

Cover and text design by Darren Holmes
Author photo on page 64 by David Grosfield
Cover photo by Adalberto Rios Szalay

The publication of *Among Ruins* has been generously supported by The Canada Council for the Arts.

The Canada Council for the Arts
Le Conseil des Arts du Canada

Mansfield Press Inc.
25 MANSFIELD AVENUE, TORONTO, ONTARIO, CANADA, M6J 2A9
Publisher: Denis De Klerck

for Beryl-Ann
1959-1998

Definition of the Human Subject

There are No Conquered Cities

As the Sky went Red

Hell and destruction are never full;
so the eyes of man are never satisfied.

Proverbs 27:20

Definition of the Human Subject

The term "subject" signifies any person who is a source
of raw or unformulated data and who is not acting as,
or assisting, the principal investigator.
(found poem)

BELLY OF THE BEAST

The mouth of the whale
Was so vast
And beautifully made
With its throat formed
So perfectly to the shape
Of a man
That when it closed
I did not feel
A thing.

Welcome, someone said behind me.

NERO

Rome burns under the hands of my fiddle.
There is no music for this
        That I cannot create.
Flames sing to an audience of stars,
The river hisses a low brass counter melody.
        The senate, the palaces,
The market square, the garrison houses,
The vomitorium, all crumble in a chorus
        Of scorched marble, blackened arches.
The harmony of the dying is in tune
With the harmony of the killing.

Mother, mother
I have secured your vacancy at last.
Sister, wife
Grapes are sweeter when grown
From your grave though
The Praetorian Guard has deserted.

First the Reichstag burned to the ground,
Then the air was a confetti of shattered glass.
        I would be the destroyer
Of cities under the outstretched arm of my salute,
The maker of maps over a clean, cratered land.
        Still the hidebound Russians
Could flake their flints and folkdance closer
To the frozen earth. In Dresden bodies char
        Like paper in the mangled architecture
And a thousand years shall end here
With the final movement of a finger on a trigger.

Wife of a day
Our blood has mixed on the marriage certificate.
Loyal servants
The needle scratches out Wagner in this dusty,
Stale bunker under blasted Berlin,
The last border of my Reich.

Crystal glasses tink together while hands shake
In rhythm at the Press Club. Spin doctors
       Compose the usual tales
And a pious face assures the cameras
That while Los Angeles burns to its own
       Redundant beat, the tune
Is not catching, its echo confinable
And California no place for revolutions.
       But I am a naked man beneath
My suit and soon a hostile savage drumming
Fills the Lincoln bedroom.

Wife, companion
My other women are calling and I listen
Because they are not you.
Young mistress, you will leave me also
When these clumsy fingers
No longer make music.

COUGHING UP BLOOD

I cannot be deceived in that
Colour; that drop of blood
Is my death warrant.
I must die.
                            ~John Keats

So, I am a poet now.

I have developed a rare and
Ingenious talent. In the frozen
Heart of January I can spit summer
Roses in the sink,
Letting them ooze, trailing sickly stems
Toward the drain, a souvenir,

A loss for words. A silent fear
Of the staring spectre whose wide
Blood eyes gaze out
From the upturned skull and
Slide into its mouth, like bleeding
Yolks of foetus eggs laid out

For my consumption. Red wine
And Tylenol, water gums and powder
Teeth; a mouth without resistance.
I am a high stakes fever, the jumbled
Nerves; a snake-eyed lizard
Of twitches who stares from the mirror

And learns the euphoria
Of having no fingers. Adam's lead
Apple, a world of substance
Wedged in my neck, a meal for a
Python, swallowed whole and
Spitting skin and skeletons, I pick

My teeth with ribs of rats.
A choked faucet dripping poppy
Syrup, my popping cherry throat
Drops bruises on the porcelain. I am
Too full, overflowing, an abandoned
Kettle spending itself in spurts

And shudders. Ignoring
The numb slowly crawling
Down my paper entrails, I turn
The cold tap, wash the wounds down
The cold pipe and fumble with the drain.
I sweat in cold places, the surface

Of water. A funeral pall.

Once there was a creature
Who saw trees and invented axes,
Stood on mountains and demanded a shovel,
Looked upon deer and dreamed of arrows,
Gazed at the sky and thought: *bombers.*
Who saw himself in the pool and said: God,

it must be God, only God in all of nature dissects.

He kept up the process
Of invention: thumbs begat thumbscrews,
Skin meant fire, for feet the bastinado,
Splints for the legs, the strappado
Conducted like a gravity test.

To walk through fields of blood, he gave himself honour.
Armies meant gun powder which meant larger armies
Which meant artillery until he planted enough parts
In the dirt that the earth grew wicked
And the ocean was littered with his purpose.

For once he knew the glorious sensation of dying
For a cause, he became quiet and kept working.

> Wives were made, then widows.
> On a house by the shore, she watches
> With grey eyes and wind-swept hair,
> Surveying the pitiless water.
> For nine years of twilights,
> She has stood like this.

Him, A Stranger

As a final love letter to the casket
She peered inside,
Placed a hand mirror on the body
As she has always done
At strange funerals.

As with others defined
By what has been buried
And made monumental,
She has fields of accusing stones
To move between on sunny days

And reshape against.
The untouched dead have gone
And with them their future follies,
Leaving reasons and memories
To be judged

By her. She has known death,
Cannot understand those who make
Him a stranger, who move in crowds,
Get engaged, get married:
She has known death, walking

Past the flowers and ceremonies,
Basements and blast furnaces.
The stained glass windows
And looking glass corpses
And all that she has mourned

Watch her silently.
In remembrance
She takes a hammer,
Puts the coffin lid in place
And drives the final nails

Into her bed, kept for one body
Alone, a tight mausoleum with fresh
White linen. And after a tepid slumber,
She seeks out the latest
Broken romances from the daily papers.

LAZARUS

(after T. S. Eliot)

And I have come back to tell you
All your fears are true:
   Experts are easily mistaken,
   The milk in the fridge is rancid,
   And your wife is bedding a man
   Who smiled when he shook your hand
   At the country club or opera.
   You have a terrible hangover,
   Your lawyer is a drug addict,
   Your stocks have begun to fall,
   Your horoscope has lead you wrong
And murderers are free, against us all.
That is everything.
That is all.

And I am risen from the dead,
Calm as shock, more dead than thou
With cuticles receded and my stone
Rolled back.
   In the large and laughing market square
   You gather around with the intimation
   That my squatting posture
   Must mean I know something. With my arms
   Raised up and my thin form grown tall
I have come back to tell you
The era of prophets is over.
That is everything I can recall.
That is everything.
That is all.

Unnamed

Really just a simple question
When planted villages were sown,
Houses uprooted, the market blown
Apart and roads swarming with mercenaries;
As impaled women littered the ditches,
The pantries looted. His family worked
These fields for six generations, patched up
The same hovel (really just a simple man)
Warmed hands over the same hearth.

Outside Pristina
The fields were burnt, the hovel scorched,
The hearth cracked and he stood in his doorway,
Pitchfork in hand and a stubborn chin
When his country grew bored, then mad,
And a neighbour scrambled to leave
Some mark of his own exploded home
In the mud before heavy rain erased all their tracks,
And asked really a simple question:
What is the meaning of this?
And was answered with a riddle

Of bullets through the heart.

On Georgian Bay

(for Michael Callaghan)

Some would say these rocks
Are stark or cold, an immutable surface
That betrays a hard character, or the trees
Are bent in submission to the wind,
Bowed, conquered. Or some would say
The night sky here is a black expanse
Cluttered with predictable symbols.

I say they are waiting

Like the rattler asleep in the damp grass.
No matter how cruel the effect, or how
Gail swept the cliffs; no matter
How distant the echo
Of the tremulous voice in the forests
That without windows to shield
Me now, I can possibly hear.
No matter how far off the unkept past
That is singing, it is all still there
(It is there: we have not made it)
Waiting to lay out
Its pervasive challenge:

The stars are falling
You bastard,
Make your wish.

On the Subway after Dark

I

As the underground railway
Emerges from its worm hole,
I sit beside myself, reflected,
Bored as my image
Waiting for the end of the line.

Terse and winding, the highways go
Between the streetlights, row on row,
Rising and falling, parting and mating;
An intricate journey the train
Ignores, as it burrows straight
Under fields of concrete clover. The cars,
Trailing long eyes, fling themselves
In opposite directions
Like the uneasy answers of Einstein's equations.

II

I see all and touch nothing,
A wraith against the city.
Transparent, an elemental
Part of air, inhaled and exhausted,
Bled out like carbon
Into the mouth of darkness.
Hovering over the skyline,
The horizon as a crystal ball,
I am a poisonous eye
Shadow: a yellow ghost in yellow mist,
A fortune teller without a future.

From north to south,
A million sleeping lives pass
Through my face

Painlessly. Behind this
Fleeting world I do
Not change. I blink.

Eve sues Adam for Breach of Trust

I

The expulsion was perfectly
Legal, settled as neatly
As possible. I was
Made into a chequebook
And an overdrawn account.

There were ashes
In your eyes before you struck
The match and burned
The bridge behind you.
The fields and orchards were
Scorched by official court order
In your strategic retreat.

II

We lived in a petting zoo
Under the reproachful eye
Of the Father who art

Had not discovered
And was still a nameless thing.
We learned limits at the start

And when we learned speech
We spoke little for we were
Spoken to by many voices.

And some could sing, some
Could bray, or squeak, or snarl
Or hiss. But for us our mouths

Were obstacles long before
We learned to kiss. From the tongue
We learned that there are choices.

III

She had a kindness of sorts
For creatures I had not yet named.
For them she knelt down and prayed

'Til along came a spider who crawled
Up inside her and told her everything

She had to say. And then
I was a man of decay.

IV

Of indeterminate age, I carry
The razor from the candy apple

You fed me on a necklace.
It tickles the blood

In my veins. Father's love
Was brutal, conditional

On our perfection
When we were not made perfect.

You were not Eve, my Lilith.

I have watched a man become death.

It takes hours; this bold process,
Freezing the veins, draining
The hue of life, preparing

This public execution. It takes hours,

Languid over a dozen cups of coffee
And rot, to waste
The flesh and bring bones

To the surface. In the twilight cafe

With the dying sunlight slanting
Through the windows, casting
A jaundiced haze, holding

The dust in the air, he sat.

He watched me only. He pulled his
Fingernails from his hands, laid
Them neatly on the table

And tapped out ten little blood pools

With metronome precision. The ticking
Monotone ticking, rose from behind,
Wandered slowly up my spine, filled

The room, filled my ears, quietly

Pushing other noise away. Heartbeat
Fell in time, fell in time, filled
My ears, with metronomic fingers tapping,

Ticking, keeping time, keeping time on a dried blood table.

He struck a match. A quick flame
With a whiff of sulfur, and a lit cigarette.
Smoke curled from between yellow teeth,

An exhaled wheeze of relief,

From shriveled lips, open,
Pulling back, giving way,
For the ticking, clicking

Jaws of a nutcracker doll. As his nose

Collapsed inwards and tendons
Parted before cheekbones,
He put his sunglasses over

His eyes. His face was then a skull.

Shrinking into his clothes
As his toes rattled inside his shoes
Like a gambler's dice before the throw,

He became a bag of ribs and femurs.

It seemed the dying would be easy,
A matter of ticking time, relentless
Ticking, talking to my skin

In a language of flesh. Impassive

I ordered and paid
And paid for my time; my overtime
My overstayed welcome, my unlikely

Lifetime, my invitation to leave.

The Impressionist

See me here: the soldier, the gentleman,
  the rugged explorer, the captain of industry,
  the butcher with tough hands cutting meat.
  I tenderize, pull fat away from bone.
My face and mannerisms can belong to the lawyer,
  the banker, the doctor with strong
  surgical fingers (like a piano player's,
  you say) and a deft scalpel
  that guides my slices.

And here is my impression of the man you love.

See the courtship of open flowers
  in a tight fist, the tense smile,
  the gifts, chocolates on holidays;
The ring, the bent knee,
the "I do's" or whatever (you tossing
  your bouquet to the next gullible sister),
our frozen nuptials.

After the curtain drawn aside,
I pass out cigars
  (the way you bear children
  will always impress me)
  and then we get old
  as I have slipped into character,
doing impressions.

You were convinced

but the flowers,
the flowers clapped their petals in a furious applause.

Headless

(for Frank Monardo,
killed on York University grounds,
Feb. 3, 1996, 10:29 a.m.)

They go on building
The building that won't be named after you,
Putting together what tore you to pieces.
Erecting a steel framework
Where your ribs were laid open,
Putting up walls
Where your skin blackened and broke,
Creating structure
Where you were momentarily lifted
And crumpled to earth.

Your last thoughts passed unspoken.
Such things are reserved for those
Who know death is coming,
Whose final words
Have been rehearsed.

I stroll daily
Past your true grave.
I predict a plaque in your memory.
You're one of the newspaper dead,
A man without context,
A name seeking sympathy.

My indifference is simple:
I do not know you.
We are headless
You and I.

THE BODY POLITIC OF CANADA

It was flawed in the conception.

The proud and hateful parents
Soon regretted their union, quick
As it was, a fumbled groping in a small
Village after too much whiskey. Its history
Began in a few missing periods.
The pregnancy continued, a time
Of nausea and mood swings and sickness,
As the fragile embryo matured
With rampant cell division and
The hard stomach stretched
Farther and farther out. The parents
Fought and drank, ignoring the forced
Labour. Until the water broke.

Born as Siamese Twins

It shared a coat
Of skin, fluids running
Through common organs,
It was propped up for
Display on the same skeletal
Frame; its blood river-rushed
Through a single
Heart. But it was of two
Heads: it listened to distinct
Voices, spoke in different
Tongues to unlike icons,
And cast its sight
In opposing directions.

When Siamese Twins are separated

Often one dies, while the other
Grows up weak and teetering,
Its balance shaking, hips clicking,
Its loss permanent like it has no shadow.
The sense of loss maddening, a hole,
A cut heart, blood denied
The dead half.
                              A punishing anxiety,
Leaves it with timid hands
Stuck in pockets and constant glances
Over the shoulder, seeking the twin
No longer there and running palms
Over a belly full of scars.

THE PRISONER'S STATEMENT

On Friday
At one minute past midnight
I will be executed
For crimes against democracy.

You see, I neglected to vote
In the race for mayor,
Brought back undeclared
Liquor from the tropics, was seen
In public in a group
Of three or more; I stayed
Under 'no loitering' signs
And talked freely of politics
While my taxes and parking
Tickets went unpaid.

As the hour draws near
That shall soon make me dead
They send priest upon preacher
In hope that remorse
Is my permanent feature,
So they can forgive me before
They cut off my head.

But I shall tip
My wide-brimmed hat
To accusing lords
Under election banners
When I am
The last man killed
On the steps
Of parliament hill
Who shares a joke
With his executioner.

You will never see him coming, or know
Who conjured this night dancer
                From the primordial mist
To take you. You will barely
Notice his hands at work in place
Of your own. It will seem your feet step
Over the ragmen as you descend
To the subway. His desires seem
Right enough: acquisition, torment,
                Pleasure.
You will think it is you that pawn things
You vowed never to lose and sign
Your will in his forgotten name.
You might never meet him face to face or endure
The dazzling pleasure his flesh
                Can accommodate
Once your servitude has been devised.
There is no vacation you can take
To flee; no amount of Dominican rum
Can drown him, nor any
Sleek dark whore satisfy
                His crushing momentum
Once it is in motion. No cloth
Across your brow can soothe
His burning fever.
                Rejoice, my friend,
For should the demon choose
Not to unmake thee
Thou shalt never emerge to thy true vocation.

HELEN

(for Helen Kalogiros, wherever she may be)

She slips a cigarette
From the package, rows
Of white columns in strong
Hands; a respite from
Romantic yearnings
And other such speculations
About her character.
Exalted much and much
Disparaged. Her hair, a mantle of envy
Wrapped about her, a defense
As much as an attraction.
Hazel eyes linger a wistful
Moment on the small flame
In her hand, a quick reflection
And a memory of burning towers
Snuffed out by the motion
Of a thumb. She says
Her father never calls
But watches over her
Through her brother, who
Sees him every other Sunday.
Bored in a frostbitten nation where
No men would wage war for her
Or even think of doing so, she turns
Her face to the East while the sun sets
Behind. With the rolling, cold
Ocean between her and Greece, a home
Where she swims in the sea and is thrown
Out of Orthodox churches, she moves
Through a moribund city
Without history compared to her.

Like him those who remain are drunk
Or stupid, not so much willing to stay
But unable to leave when the storm
Unburdens the land of its inhabitants.
It is the tempest's temptation to hold him,
Fool him until he thinks
It is the sky that hates, not I.

On grey beaches
He paces along the rocks,
Deck shoes clumped with sand
And clouds crowded around his head,
His wife fled inland. To redeem
Himself for years of inactivity
As an anvil to the wind

He would survive it: survive his home
Torn from its moorings, survive the gusts
That rip up pavement and the thirty-foot
Wall of water that shambles from the gulf
Like a fairy tale ogre. Survive
When the shore, the ocean, the docks,
And the clouds shatter into one,

Survive the merciless onslaught
        of the sky
And quietly sink in the swirling eddy
        of the eye.

The Pariah

Young mothers in the park
Smell something ill-born about him,
Bundle up their charges and move on.

Skilled labourers sense
His clumsiness and laugh uneasily,
Aware of the danger.

Lovers, flushed with wine,
Intuit the cold eunuch, pack
Their blanket lunch and rush home to bed.

An old woman observes the pass
Of his rickety shadow across the sun
And wonders if he is the agent she waits for.

A doctor retreats before the hooded eyes
Bubbled under white eyelids, cuts short his break
And, back turned, mutters, *a cure, a cure.*

The statues of dead kings remain
Impassive to this plainly human drama.

THE SEX-LIFE OF LAB RATS.

The sex-life of scientists is wild and cruel,
A rabid flailing of bodies

On a clean tile floor. Unplanned,
The uproar consumes

The dinner hour, hunger racing
Along the walls. Experiments neglected

Among the tubes and pumps, as the clawing
And the pawing disturbs the sanitary air.

The sex-life of lab rats is foreign and precise,
One body courteously mounting another

In a maze of possibilities. Empirical
Exploration, clothes folded neatly,

The liaison entered in the day
Planner. The project was a success,

They said; copulation occurred
Before time ran out.

Half Lives

I've felt the sun
Of orange mornings
As time wound up.

I've committed tax fraud
With the best of intentions.

I've plucked fruit
From trees in ancient gardens
While hanging in air.

Even cured cancer and forgotten.

In my naked and skeletal rage
I breathed fire and ash,
Granted death in frozen postures.

I've trod on the outline
Of a women where she lay back
And felt her
Seismic shudders in my feet.

And risen to walk, meaning
I've died a hundred times over.

BLIND,

We read each other like Braille,
Decoding messages written on skin,

Trying to read beneath.

She plays ribs like piano keys,
Unlocking tune with slow touches,

Trying to read beneath.

We trace our eyes with fingertips
The way the blind touch faces,

Trying to read beneath.

We tap each other's skeletons
In a Morse Code distress call

Before a little death drags us down.

In the dark she is an octopus
All hands and still seeking,
Bestowing pleasure on more points
Than should be possible
For two small hands and ten thin digits.

For once the words between us
Are sensations, are silent, heard
By nerves and trembling in the blood.

This act:

This interlocking of stick figures
        in a dark room drained of the world,

This knocking of dark hands on darkness' door,

This twining of black roses in the garden of night,

This fornication of scorpions
      on a bone frame bed,

Shall preserve us as we grope to be whole.

There are No Conquered Cities

There are No Conquered Cities

Why should that city, defenseless and pure as the wedding necklace
Of a forgotten tribe, keep offering itself to me?

~Czeslaw Milosz

I

Go then, tell the ancient cities of your need.
Allow them to overcome you.

React to their demise
As when Troy was burning,
The lofty flames kissing your eyelids.

II

For every era an encompassing architect
Traces holy patterns in the dirt,
Genuflects at this foundation. To the caves

Of prehistory cling paintings of unnamed cities
On fire, towers broken and men put to the spear.
There were no cities then but madmen and shamans

Knew what to expect. The Vatican archive
Holds a millennium of plans for unbuilt centres,
Designs for Augustine's metropolis

Of the mind, his viewpoint of the damned,
His powerhouse of worship. For every era
A child builds a sandcastle.

He works knowing
There is nothing worth doing without the potential for harm.

III

Uruk has fallen.
Babylon has fallen.
Atlantis rolls beneath the waves.
Jericho's walls broken before the blast of a trumpet.

Some lean from their windows.
Some walk cautiously to work or deal in black market
Cigarettes; some creep to market under sniper fire,
Some roll in bed in the afternoon sun, then
The roar of Allied jets or the shadow
Of the hand of God and nothing.

If war is politics by other means,
Victory is a clutching hand outstretched,
The moment when life becomes
A whim of a conquering general,
When goods and slaves of defeat
Can be simply wasted. Fingers reach out
In the wreck of a home. Drums are silenced
At the point of dissolution.

They are here. They are at the gates.
They are at the gates of Constantinople.

IV

Divided cities,
The thank-you cards
Of fallen empires.

V

Freedom has different names
At the nexus of a civil war

Where a high concrete wall
Forms the precise wording of liberation.

In the sentry tower of the Brandenburg Gate, where
For every action there is an opposing ideology,

It is not like the Coney Island of the mind,
But the metropolis of Faust

Where souls were sold for information, and to be or not to be
Was not a question but an equation unsolvable,

Under the sights of the Grepos. Where von Karajan
Made his stand playing Beethoven beneath the old Teutonic sky.

That was the white flag of victory. Thirteen years
After the final notes have fallen, the Wall

Collected for souvenirs, the movement is clean and easy,
The sentry another useless object of art admired

By gawkers as they pass. Sides are outdated
In the bold realm of the new German coin toss

And the Brandenburg Gate, once risen, once fallen,
Stands faithless, bereft of its meaning.

VI

For days after Christmas
Charcoal grey clouds
Assembled above Montreal,
A divided parliament,

Until two systems clashed
And the rain of ice began. For five full
Days the angry sleet did not relent,
Street signs were bowed and bent

Regardless of Language Laws. The sky
Howled like a wounded animal.
By the second day trees were hunched
Over every road in a series of crippled archways.

Hydro towers crumpled,
A child's playthings after a tantrum,
Cutting a swath of darkness
Through la belle province.

On the third day of the reign of ice
The cross on Mont Royal went out.

At the fifth day some were convinced
The clouds were not joking,
The apocalypse was finally here
And Notre Dame Basilica no place to hide.

By the end of the week the work of the storm
Was over and the sun emerged
Over an immutable artifact of glass
Too bright to look upon.

Parc Lafontaine glowed for miles,
Its fountain frozen in place.
The church bells and the crystal city
Beckoned us, raw and finally equal.

VII

Ode to Joy:

Outside Roy Thompson Hall,
Pity for the composer
Because the piece was written
After his deafness.
Shame he never heard it, a man
Breathes in January air,
Adjusts his cufflinks.
A wife, stray blonde strands,
Nods agreement, hails a cab.

Around them trees clutch at winter fog,
The a cappella of machinery drones on and on and on.

VIII

More than ten years dead
And I hadn't thought of you
Until you came in a dream,
Aged hardly a day since the accident
But O your eyes were grey.

Hello, my friend.

You went away.

Yes, far away.

Where have you been?

I have been diving. A long time. A long way down.

What have you seen?

I think I died at Troy, the long ash spear knocked from my hands,
The bronze armour stripped from my shoulders.

Our table is empty without you.

I think I died at Rhodes under the sword of a whirling dervish,
Blazing with hashish.

The home fires burn in your absence.

I think I died at Ladysmith where I understood nothing but a bloody flag
And God Save the Queen.

For weeks we could not utter your name.

I think I died in heaping wreckage, the steering wheel welded to my chest.

We played songs in the early hours.

I think I died.

The last time we spoke you were determined fate could be thwarted,
And you said to me—
"Still you might come back."

The cities of the mind do not perish.

IX

Come then, tell the modern cities of your need.
Always come back to them. Seed
Your gardens elsewhere, watch the sunrise
Elsewhere. Lay your imagination before them
Like an untouched canvas under the brush.
Here you will find no consolation
Not of your own making. Remake it.
Impress yourself hard on it as it shapes you anew

And say this concrete, too, is beautiful
For generations of feet stride upon it,
And this lamppost, this dark alley, this park bench,
These stray cats, and these flowers in a window box.
The wall of names of the war dead is beautiful.
In the silver July moonlight
I am a shoeless dancer over broken glass. The city takes in breath.
And holds. And I live *here*.

Vienna is founded.
London and Paris mark their ascension.
Leningrad breaks the siege.
Dresden rebuilt from a black husk.
And some human thoughts of Atlantis are stirring far away waters.

X

A watchman in Mariacki
Tower, seeing the Tartars approach,
Raised his trumpet to sound a warning
And was rewarded with an arrow through the throat.

Every day a trumpeter ascends
The winding steps to repeat the song,
Stops at the moment of his predecessor's death.
Krakow is held fast, lifted with a single resounding note.

XI

They come into the blank desert,
Western men with shovels, dust brushes and grants,
Foreigners in Bermuda shorts and Tilley hats
Reap spoils from the long-suffering earth
As the sun picks their brains clean.

They come in search of Sodom and Gomorrah.
What did the market square look like?
City hall? A theatre? They are curious to see inns
For wayward travellers. The main wells,
An irrigation system will come visible.
Finally, the prison excites them
For what did one do to get imprisoned in Sodom?

What they don't know, these late Victorian
Hobbyists, is that I was here first; I or someone
Like me, has always been here first
Without map or compass

And carries Sodom and Gomorrah away in a suitcase.

Miles from the digging sites,
My Bedouin guide said
Once there was a city here,
Drowned by God in a rain of fire.

I sniffed the air
                    and a faint taste of salt
Replied, No
                    there is still a city here.

XII

Agamemnon roars, the fall
Of Troy assured, his war is won.
High on the rampart walls
Brilliant Hektor holds his infant son.

After the blood and sweat
Of a thousand armies has settled,
The dust stirs by a thousand yet
Who raise their swords to test their mettle.

Even among the slaughter
There is other work to be done;
We can redress the wrongs

So long as Demodokos sings the song
And some lift the wine and peal the laughter
Or walk among the ruins.

As the Sky went Red

ORIGAMI

In the room where you keep her
She works by candlelight,

Folding a piece of rice paper over and over
Onto itself.
       When it is done
She looks up and hands you the weightless bauble,
An octahedron.

What is it?

It is your heart.

THE STRAIGHT MAN CRACKS A SMILE

When your third wife threw you out
With your porn mags
And whiskey bottles,
You held in the laughter.
After she called and said
You were forgiven
You stayed away
Because the whole situation
Suddenly seemed
Funny.

THE PROCEDURE

At the end of Day One
It was awful. They had to be given
Straight vodka to finish.
Most of them could barely look
And one threw up in the corner.
They had broken his knees
And ankles with hammers.

Day Two wasn't much better.
They were instructed to cut off
His arms at the elbows
Then cauterize the stumps with blowtorches.
The amount of blood was enormous
And the screaming so bad we played
Them some music. That seemed to help.

On the Third Day there was improvement
With them working as a team,
Passing their instruments back and forth
With mechanical ease
And a notable lack of nervous trembling
As they peeled off strips of his skin.
They were sleeping better.

They spoke differently and could
See themselves as other people,
Say things like "His legs needed breaking;
this was accomplished"
And chat about weather or movies
While pulling his eyes and teeth.
That was Day Four.

By Days Five and Six they seemed
A little bored and talked about
Doing continental shifts
So they might have more free time.
After they carved off his genitals
Like a reflex, they tossed their aprons
In the laundry basket without looking.

On Day Seven they went home early,
Shook themselves into their wives
Or bought dog food. Dusty bottles
In hand, they paused a moment
In their wine cellars,
Stunned. They yelled and played
With their children, and were terrified.

In Praise of the Unabomber

I

The Critics Agree:

"A fireworks exhibition of fantasy, sexual love, and moral awareness."
~*The New York Times Book Review*

"The essay's devastatingly sustained black irony stands comparison with Swift's *A Modest Proposal*. It is, I think, the Unabomber's finest achievement to date."
~*The Financial Times*

"...enormous fun...The Unabomber has found a fresh way to orchestrate the themes of American innocence, energy, and inchoate ambition...A remarkable achievement."
~*Newsweek*

"The effect is a cross between a long scream, a nervous breakdown and a Tacitean indictment of a regime."
~*The London Times*

II

There are, of course,
easier ways to get published
but few quite as innovative.

The Times and *The Post* are nothing
to scoff at and
he was the only writer
to be on *People's* 25
most interesting list
that year.

His friends and relatives
often wondered about him
so concerned with letters.
What a strange character
they would say,
an even stranger sentence to pronounce.

Beneath the sagging roof
The stylist has taken shelter
in the unlikely
guise of a bitter
failure in order
to elude the FBI
and other censorship agencies.

Now tried and convicted
for beliefs so dangerous
not even PEN International
dare write letters on his behalf.

III

FBI Profile of the Disgruntled Scribbler:

He would most likely be a loner with few ties to family or loved ones.
Probably has travelled extensively in the country of his origin but rarely
outside of it. Would travel alone and avoid open, crowded areas, almost
always preferring movement after nightfall. Uncomfortable in the glare
of headlights. Excessively jealous and possessive, and highly
demanding of acquaintances and lovers. Likely to have come from a
broken home with uncertain, or illegitimate, parentage. Severe anti-
establishment tendencies. Talks to a presence who is not there and
frequently complains of voices or other people living in his head.
Overactive imagination with a tendency to hyperfocus. Better at division
than multiplication. Plagued by feelings of uselessness masked by an
excessive, almost comic, egotism. Severe feelings of persecution.
Prefers old globes to new maps. Devours the world with the senses, a
state where all things are part of the search for balance, order. Is
attracted to images of women in jeopardy. Picks his targets on the basis
of their usefulness to him. He seeks to own them, ingest some parts of
them so as to claim their spirit, or essence, as trophy. Does not believe
in coincidence but willing to exploit it. Most likely, he is a failure.

IV

Under his hands it takes shape.
The smaller he makes it the bigger it breaks,
the better it scatters.

It is easy then
to become the sort of writer
who sees the world
as a series of targets.

Rarely, he would think
of how all this might
be received, how people
will react (new ideas
always finding resistance)
and if his works will
earn him a part of history
from a time that passed him by,
before addressing
his latest piece of black mail.

He hears an engine all around him
chugging out a juggernaut mantra:
makeitnewmakeitnewmakeitnewmakeitnew.

STILLBIRTH MACHINE I

This is a solid
Grey landscape of penetration,
Of violence
In stasis,
Of having no eyes or
Eyelids, of the endless pain

of beauty

A paralyzed moment
        of motion as

hands become
 gears become
  spine become
   vanished become
    veins become
     hydraulic become
      nipples become
       machines become

knees become
 lips become
  flesh become
   wrists become
    fingers become
     needles become
      cunt become
       death become

        her

The aged infant born
Dead, its supple
Mother spread
On a bed of

afterbirth

Stillbirth Machine II

In this: flesh operates
On itself,

Installs upon its skin
All the features of Mother Earth:

Rats, teeth, knuckles, a gnawed-off
Ear, waves of worms, an engine,

And most of all, the pulverized mass
Of misshapen children panting
For her teats, waiting

To kill her in the name
Of still life. Legs raised

And open for death, a boy,
She can not remember whether
He is entering or leaving her.
She can only pray:

I have a birthing in mind.

O my creator
Grant me the gears to get the job done.

One glimpse is all it takes
  before you become
  a candidate for many things:
  statistics and martyrdom among them.
One glimpse is all it takes
  before it dances and dances
  in the corners of your eyes
  and you see the front
  grills of trucks or the wheels
  of streetcars and know
  that they too have appeal.

One glimpse is all it takes
  as a succulent rage enfolds you
  and such a strange hurt holds you
  that you believe in words like *cursed*.
One glimpse is all it takes
  to send you howling down back streets,
  a grey man exhaling dust
  and soon you'll try to embrace the ocean.

One glimpse is all it takes
  to wreck you for a lifetime.

Taking Down Directions to Hell

"After filling out the appropriate forms
Purchase a ticket by credit card,
Enter the station at 11:30 in the evening
And board the bus.

After the departure, relax,
The trip will go smoothly.

Read an entertainment magazine
Or a cheap thriller, imagining yourself
To be something else. Remove
Your watch and sleep. Die
If you have to. Or
Simply stare at nothing out the window.

Take your wife and children
Out of your wallet and burn them.
Matches will be provided.

Make a mould of your heart,
Cast it in iron and fill it with chocolates,
Then send it to someone you once knew.

You will come to believe in your own perfection.

Upon your return, you will find the house empty.
Take the money off the table,
Go find yourself a woman
And try to have a good time."

Sinews stiffen, blood dries
In footprints across the stage,
A man becomes 'the body.'

So arrangements are made,
The comforting ritual of it all:
The calculated gloom
Of the procession
That empties the theatre. The body
Is taken somewhere.

Mourning is a slow grapple with an unseen foe.
While the body sprouts
Shoots and becomes a garden bed
Of potatoes, there is still no dialogue
To fill the space after the yawning

'because'

There is something in the thought
Of being 'found dead'
That I find remotely appealing.

The sky was black when it happened,
Black as blood in the moonlight.
The shore I do not remember,
Whether sand or stones.
The time I do not remember,
The seasons were moving,
Away.

Only the pull I remember,
The voices in the waves
Speaking a language that bones
Understand like a whisper in the lungs.

Come down Saint Christopher,
She has left but we remain.
Come drown, lie with us, hung
With the dead men who drink forever.
You'll like it here.
You can leave behind the pain of breathing.
Delicious martyr,
Bleed like the moon in the blacklight.

There, on sand or stones
My littoral feet held me
From my brothers among the dead,
Drawn down and wrapped in quiet arms,
Their visions seeped out like ichor
That blackened the moon in the bloodlight
Where I stood crying as the sky went red.

On the bleeding plains of Asia
I lifted my first coat from the body
Of a member of the Golden Horde.

      The year was 1239.
      And I was young then.

In 1535 a man beheaded for obstinacy
And faith bestowed me his boots
Because he wished to walk
Barefoot to the block.
From him I grew
A few inches
In height.

These shirts were supplied
Wholesale from the noted tailors
Of Austerlitz, Jena, and Sons,
Each the same cut with slight
Variations in the stitching.

      Back at the front
      I commanded and I served
      With the monogram
      Of another emperor
      Over my heart.

The cane
With the brooding thunder
  lizard curled around its shaft
  was purchased in London
  at the turn
    of the century.
Its metal tip clicked hollow
  against the cobblestone
  past the shoes
  of the city's rich
    and the city's poor.
The dragon nestled in my hand
  brewed fire in its belly
  and touched muzzles
  with its brother
    sleeping in my blood.

  My other coat (the leather one—
  double breasted with a fur collar)
Came from the remains of a downed
German pilot in Versailles. From the style
  of corpse he presented, I could tell
  that he had earned his wings
  & his fame & his cross & his place
  in the grave.

      I shook the body out of the garment
      And kept walking. It was 1918. Soon,
      I thought, this will all be over.
      We shall no longer dress like gentlemen.

There is a trail
Of fingerless bodies
Left in my long wake.
And now I wear ten rings.

We took from women and children then.
They came to us, huddled masses
  herded off the trains
  and gave us everything:
  their suitcases, clothes,
  shoes, hair and jewellery.
Their bones were sent for study
  at the Natural Science Museum of Berlin
  to see if they were as human as they claimed.

          We hoarded wealth and hung many lives
          On our flypaper skin.
          We saved the portraits and killed
          The people, admired the technique
          But not the form.

          As old as we were
          It felt, for a last moment,
          Like it was fresh. We had
          Washed ourselves clean
          And written a necrology
          In soap
                    and ashes.

          I often wondered who could blame me
          For having such stars fixed in my eyes?

Shuffling, stiff-kneed,
  around a sterile basement,
  (the dead all about me, neatly laid out
  as folded laundry) I take
  what gold fillings I can find,
  leftover wedding rings
  or medals from the veterans.
These days the bodies are well prepared,
  suits open in back, but sewn in front
  to keep up appearances.
Each of these people is a "Y"
  of stitching. My occupation
  buried their questions.

I sought for something
Among the carnage of the fallen;
  some precious wisdom
  from those wounds.
With what was left I found
  it simple to seek cover, to infiltrate,
  anonymous, in any daily uniform,
These bored and stylish kingdoms
Which fall in and out of favour,
  on the tastes of the moment.

Memento Mori

At one point late in the evening
You put down your drink,
Hugged yourself,
And shivered.

I feel like someone just stepped on my grave.

How we laughed

then.

ACKNOWLEDGEMENTS:

I would like to thank first of all my family and friends, including my
mother, Eleanor; my siblings, Louise, Jim, Donna, & Beryl (R.I.P);
shannon bramer and Dave Derry; Barry Callaghan and Claire
Weissman Wilks; David and Annie Layton; and Samantha Zacher.

Many thanks are also due to my publisher Denis De Klerck and teacher
Richard Teleky for their editorial acumen and great encouragement
regarding the preparation and culmination of this manuscript.

Some of these poems first appeared in *Exile—The Literary Quarterly,*
The Literary Review of Canada, The Queen Street Quarterly, and *beetred—*
a journal of poetry. Thanks to the editors.

Note: Stillbirth Machine I & II were inspired by paintings of the
same names by the Swiss surrealist H. R. Giger. They can be found
in his *Necronomicon.*

Finally, this book would not have been possible without the love
and support of Priscila Uppal, for whom no blazon could ever be
good enough.

CHRISTOPHER DODA
lives and writes in Toronto.